Made in United States
Orlando, FL
18 October 2022

23603955R00055